Washington Elementary 2009

A Collection of Student Poetry

1st WORLD
PUBLISHING

Washington Elementary
2009
A Collection of Student Poetry

© 1st World Library - Literary Society, 2009
P. O. Box 2211, Fairfield, Iowa 52556
• Tel: 641-209-5000 • Fax: 866-440 5234
• Web: www.1stworldlibrary.com

First Edition

LCCN: 2009927912

ISBN: 978-1-4218-9094-4

Editing: Aman and Anya Charles

Foreword

It is with great pleasure and pride in our students that we present this compilation of student work. We hope that the families of our students and other audiences enjoy the efforts and creativity that our students have displayed in creating this book.

My sincere thanks to our teachers who do a wonderful job for our students, and who were enthusiastic about this opportunity to showcase their students' work in this manner. We also give great thanks to Rodney and Anya Charles for being so supportive in making this opportunity available to our students.

Student writing is an integral part of the language arts curriculum. Reading and writing are complementary processes, and both are imperative in order for our students to become truly literate adults. Our teachers seek opportunities for our students to engage in authentic writing tasks that motivate their very best efforts. This writing activity exemplifies this concept of student writing for an authentic purpose.

Incorporating poetry in reading and writing instruction has always been a mainstay in the language arts. As we have gained knowledge through professional development, our faculty has become even more aware of the benefits of poetry to their instruction. The lower grades benefit from the phonemic, phonic, and rhyming elements of poetry which are paramount in the learning to read process. In the upper grades, poetry enhances the students' use of words, their vocabulary development, and their enjoyment of literature. At all levels, poetry can be effectively used to improve reading fluency.

We hope that you enjoy these poems from our students. As you read the poems, you will certainly be optimistic about the great promise that the future holds for these wonderful kids!

Joe Carr
Principal
Washington Elementary

Introduction

Washington Elementary School staff is appreciative that 1st World Library provided our students with the opportunity of becoming published authors. Our students were excited about getting their poems published. A variety of styles were used. Some rhymed, some had a specific number of words or syllables per line, and some were whatever the students wanted them to be. Poetry is hard to define. One thing for certain is that each poem belongs to the child who wrote it. We hope you enjoy this small glimpse of the students that we see every day.

Sharon Leach,
5th grade teacher

Me

Alex
Loves football
Eats junk food
Xciting

Loves Nascar fans only
Apple
Nascar racing
Does tricks
On my bike
Nice

Happy-go-lucky
Alex
Helpful
Not an only child

Alex Landon-Hahn

My Cat Ozzy

My cat's name is Ozzy.

He is big, cute, and fozzy.

He loves to eat kitty chow but nothing that tastes mozzy.

When it gets cold and frosty, Ozzy cuddles with his brother to be warm and cozzy.

And when you're at the door waiting no matter how frosty, when I see you I put out your food and say, "I love you Ozzy." And I know you love me too.

Cade

Super Sally

Super Sally
sat with Sammie
sitting
super silly.

Cheyenne Anderson

Spring

Flowers blooming, Birds are singing
What a beautiful sight
Bunnies hopping in the meadow
Oh, What a delight
The spring air so fresh and clean,
Having more fun than you need.
Why are you in the tree?
Be careful don't fall…Not again!
Now I have to spend my spring in a sling!

Chloe Spalla

Fall

Fall is warm,
I see leaves fall from trees
and cover the ground
then next is cold weather
and winter comes.

Chris Harris

Cheetahs

Cheetahs are fast
Cheetahs are fascinating
Cheetahs are polka-dotted

Chris McDaniel

The Hairball

Oh, Bobby ate a hairball,
He mistook it for spaghetti,
And then he puked it down an elevator shaft,
And here came poor old Eddie,

Now you see, poor old Eddie had no hair,
If you asked he'd probably say he didn't care,
But then the old hairball, it came plummeting
down,
Even before Eddie could even make a sound,
Old Eddie had some hair.

Cooper Dodd

"The Apple"

```
                    ss
                    tt
                    ee
                    mm
          apple apple apple apple
        munch munch munch munch
       red yellow green red yellow green
      crunch crunch crunch crunch crunch crunch
     yum yum yum yum yum yum yum yum yum yum
    apple apple apple apple apple apple apple apple apple apple
   munch munch munch munch munch munch munch munch
  red yellow green red yellow green red yellow green red yellow
 crunch crunch crunch crunch crunch crunch crunch crunch crunch
 yum yum yum yum yum yum yum yum yum yum yum yum yum yum
 apple apple apple apple apple apple apple apple apple apple apple apple
 munch munch munch  worm worm worm worm yuk yuk yuk yuk yuk
 red yellow green red yellow worm worm worm yuk yuk yuk yuk yuk yuk
 crunch crunch crunch crunch crunch crunch crunch crunch crunch crunch
 yum yum yum yum yum yum yum yum yum yum yum yum yum yum yum
 apple apple apple apple apple apple apple apple apple apple apple apple apple
 munch munch munch munch munch munch munch munch munch munch munch
 red yellow green red yellow green red yellow green red yellow green red green
 crunch crunch crunch crunch crunch crunch crunch crunch crunch crunch
 yum yum yum yum yum yum yum yum yum yum yum yum yum yum
  apple apple apple apple apple apple apple apple apple apple apple apple
   munch munch munch munch munch munch munch munch munch
    red yellow green red yellow green red yellow green red yellow
     crunch crunch crunch crunch crunch crunch crunch crunch
      yum yum yum yum yum yum yum yum yum yum yum
       apple apple apple apple apple apple apple apple
        munch munch munch munch munch
          red yellow green red yellow
```

Dakota Andersen

12

Lime Green

Lime green is the color of my flip-flops
Lime green is the color of limes
The leaves of the trees are lime green
Lime green is the color of my pants
An apple is lime green
You can color anything lime green

Gabrielle Kuehl

Spring

Springtime is fun time
Raining and pouring on you
And beautiful fun

Gavin Stever

Football Season

Fun to play with friends
Out of bounds
Off sides
Touch down
Beat up
All for one
Losing the game
Lining up for the game
Season over
Eaten up
Ain't giving up
Surrounding you
Off the air
Now over the game

Hunter Symmonds

The Wizard

The Wizard he is good or bad
The Wizard has a very great dad
The Wizard was running on a treadmill one day
The Wizard turned it to 720 some way
The Wizard he tripped, he fell, and he slipped
The Wizard he then landed on his bed
The Wizard he got up and said
The Wizard's time to change thy beard!

Jacob Smithburg

The Vase

Once there was a boy named Eddy Frinquetty.
Eddy loved to play outside,
but unfortunately it was raining.
He sat by the window bored and alone
he had an idea
something he could play alone.
He got a bat, a ball, and his helmet,
his favorite of all.
He threw up the ball and it made a sound making
the dog squall,
and the worst of all
it hit the vase which his mother didn't like at all.

John Fleig

Me Myself and I

Kittens are what she likes.
Irritated sometimes.
Enjoys being outdoors.
Really likes her friend Lura.
An animal lover at heart.

Never really enjoys school, only sometimes.
Laughs way too much.
She is a very sociable person.
Only enjoys being inside sometimes.
Never wants to live in town she enjoys farms.

Even though she lives
in a small town.

Kiera

I Love Hobos

HOBOS DON'T HAVE A HOME
HOBOS LIVE IN ALLEYS
HOBOS DON'T HAVE A LOT OF FOOD
HOBOS DON'T GO TO SCHOOL
HOBOS ARE SO COOL
HOBOS CHOOSE WHERE THEY SLEEP
BUT THEY DON'T HAVE CABLE!!!!!

Kyleigh Jeffrey

The Cat Goofy

There once was a cat who got in the trash and found a hat. The hat said, "I am a bat, don't touch me."

The cat didn't say anything, it just meowed. The bat that had the hat said, "Don't just sit there and just meow, that is lame!" and the cat started singing the song Fame.

He said "You should remember my name..." (he held it out in a high voice)

Mackenzi Harwood

My Weather Haikus

When it is sunny
I want to go out and play
That makes me happy

It is cloudy out
That means it will rain later
That makes me real sad

Madison K. Lathrop

Summer

Jump in the pool
Playing Baseball
Playing Basketball
Having too much fun?
Go to the park
Hear the dog bark
Go to Florida
Go to Miami
But hurry before…
SUMMER'S OVER!

Nathan Thompson

My name

T tiny tater tot
A amazing, awesome
Y young, yellow
L little, loud, lucky
O October, outgoing
R runt, runs, rough

Taylor Ferrel

Dogs

I like dogs
They are fun to play with
Dogs are very protective
They like being taken on a walk
I wish dogs could talk
They like to sleep with you
Dogs are very cute
They can find people who are hurt
They can run fast
You can dress up a dog

Boy, I sure do like CATS

Trae VanTasell

Hunting

Hunting is fun.
    Hunting is great.
        Hunting is cool but make sure to be safe.

Don't be your brother.
    Don't be your sister.
        Grab a gun, and take them down.

Trevor Drish

My Dog Named Scum

My dog named Scum
is so very dumb
and he likes eating pumps
in the dumps
and he likes a girl cat
that catches rats.

Zachary Price

Pepsi

Pepsi is cool.
Pepsi is good.
Pepsi is a drink.
Pepsi has sugar.
Pepsi makes me hyper.

Alex Crile

Lily

Lily is a dog.
Lily is a troublemaker.
Lily plays all day.
Lily plays all night.
Lily plays all the time, and has a great big BITE!

Chase Kukuzke

When I'm Bored

When I'm bored, I close my door.
When I'm mad, I slam my door.
When I'm sad, I go outdoors and play until my
sadness goes.
Then I play some more.

Cyrus Milam

The meaning of Christmas

The meaning of Christmas has almost elapsed
Some people think it's for presents and caps,
But the true meaning, way down in your heart, are
gifts from the Lord, like Jesus who played a big part.
He died on the cross to save us from sin, and we
now have a chance to be born once again.

Dain Avery Nelson

My Place

My place is paintball.
My place is shooting.
My place hurts.
My place leaves a bruise.
My place is exciting.
My place is cool.
People get hurt in places like these.

Drew Stever

Yellow

Yellow is the color of my shirt.
Yellow is the color of the sun.
Yellow is the color that makes me feel happy.
Yellow is a bright pretty color
That can be anywhere,
You can color things yellow,
You can make things yellow,
You can do anything with the color yellow.

Emma Kuehl

Wind holds the world.
Wind is like a bird soaring.
Wind, please go go go!

Garret Bowermaster

Hawkeyes

Hawkeyes are a good team.
Hawkeyes fans are awesome.
Hawkeyes are the best team in the world.
Hawkeyes can beat Illinois.

Jarrett Hellweg

Homework Problem

I have homework problems.
Do you have homework problems?
Mine are….
I have 100 pieces of homework,
And 10 tests a day
Then one day,
I was doing my homework…
There was an earthquake, a light
Oh, it all was a dream.

Jordan Van Dijk

Stars

Stars are very bright and yellow.
Whenever you lay outside, you might see stars.
Stars are just like the sun, but they are smaller.
Sometimes you don't see them, but they are still up
there somewhere.

Kelsey Roberts

My Friends

My friends are awesome.
My friends are cool.
My friends like me and they don't like school.
They come over to my house and we play games,
But when we lose, we call each other names.
We might sit on the couch and watch TV.
We might watch Sponge Bob under the sea.
Sometimes we make forts and play with guns.
No matter what we do, we always have fun.

Kyle Schrobilgen

Colors

Yellow like the sun
Purple like a grape
Green like a lime
Red like school chairs
Orange like a beach ball
Blue like blueberries
Pink like a Laffy Taffy
All colors like a rainbow

Leya Haynes

Tacos

Tacos are good.
Tacos are great.
I am sad when all are ate.
But I may make more,
So tacos are good,
And I have no neighborhood,
So I don't have to share,
For all that I care.

Logan Angstead

Excuses

I was sitting at my desk
Trying to do my reading
When a big, hairy gorilla
Walked in and started eating!
He devoured everything in sight
He really went berserk
My backpack, lunchbox, pencils, books
And even my homework!
Wait, you're not believing this?
Let me try again…
In through the window
Flew an alien!
He demanded I give him my homework
He threatened me with a ray gun
Oh, you don't believe this either?
Let me try another one…
A magician hocus-pocused it?
I just ran out of time?
Wait, you said it's due *tomorrow*?
See you later! It's recess time!

Loreena Hucke

Red

Red is my favorite color.
Red is the color of blood.
Red is one of the colors of the American flag.
Red is the color of my favorite sweatshirt.

Luis Jimenez

The wind moves the clouds.
Condensation slowly falls,
Bringing rain to us.

Mackenzie Flattery

Pumpkin And Skittles

Pumpkin and Skittles are the names of my cats.
Pumpkin and Skittles are fun to watch.
Pumpkin and Skittles are different ages,
   yet they are the same in every way.
Pumpkin and Skittles are starting to shed.
Pumpkin and Skittles are inside cats.
Pumpkin and Skittles love the outdoors.
Pumpkin and Skittles love the sun.
Pumpkin and Skittles love to watch T.V.
Pumpkin and Skittles love FOOOOOODDDD.
Pumpkin and Skittles love me and you too!!!!!!!

Melissa Callan

When I Grow Up

When I grow up, I don't know what I'll be.
Who knows?
What I choose might not be right for me.
When I grow up, who knows what I'll do.
I might be someone who writes Haikus.
I might be a hiker or a biker.
Oh golly gee.
I think I'll just be me!

Paige Holderbaum

Trees

Trees are really tall.
Trees' leaves drop and change in fall.
Some trees can be small.

Price Slechta

The Hideout

The hideout is grand.
The hideout is cool.
The hideout is where I go after school.
The hideout is peaceful.
The hideout is a journey.
The hideout is nature.
The hideout is my sanctuary.

Shea Malloy

Ice Is Coming

I'm sitting here all alone
Watching the ice coming down
Hard.
I'm very sad.
My Dad is working overtime.
The sky is cleared.
I must be happy.
He is coming home.

Tristian Pohren

Poem

THE SUN IS VERY BRIGHT
WHEN YOU WAKE UP TO THE LIGHT
YOU MIGHT WAKE IN FRIGHT.

Troy

Blue

Blue is the color of a nice spring day.
Blue is the color of New York's bay.
Blue is the color of a summer sky.
Blue is the color of a blueberry pie.
Blue can be the color of a smoothie blend.
Blue is the color of the words:
THE END

Zach Martin

Washing Machine

I put clothing in the Washing Machine and I made a mistake because I did not check the pants pockets. When I opened the door I saw $300.00 in the Washing Machine! Uncle Randy asked where his $300.00 went.
The End

Alisa Jade Worth

IT

IT is cool.
IT is fun
IT likes to play, jump, and run.
IT plays chess it has to confess
No is not an answer it's always yes!
IT can see
IT can flee
IT turns out that IT is me!

AmanCharles

About My Dog

He likes Alaska
He likes to play in the snow,
He is quite furry
What Am I?

I am quite helpful
When I am old I'm quite big,
Type of quite good dog
What Am I?

It hurts really bad
It sometimes leaves a big mark,
It happens a lot
What Am I?

Brandon Smithburg

What am I?

Slithers on the ground,
Can be very venomous,
Have scales on my back

What am I?
Have a bunch of fur,
I live in Antarctica,
I am endangered.

Brian Buch

A Drink

May I have a drink?
I saw my teacher wink
Yes you may take a drink
Maybe it will help you think

Briseyda Jimenez

My Big Cat

My big cat has a rat!!!!!!!
He is too fat to have any more rats
Come on fat cat stop eating rats,
I caught you fat cat!!!

Give me that rat!!!!
You are a bad cat!
You're fat because you eat too many rats!!
STOP EATING RATS FAT CAT!!!!

Brynna Bowman

A Man named Phill

There once was a man named Phill,
who decided to take a pill.
He met a woman named Jill
and she fell off a hill.

Cameron Baumann

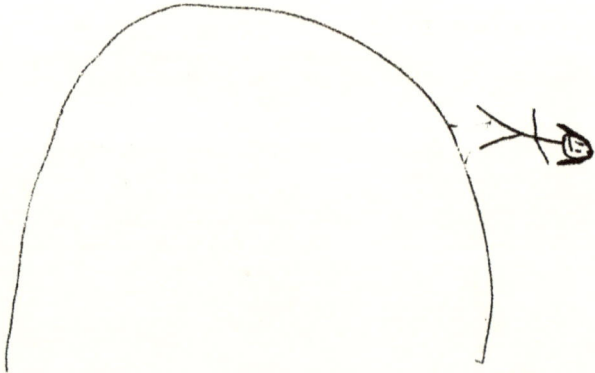

Redwoods

I walk down a gravel path
It's a foggy morning, very dim
You see a hollow tree big enough
To fit three or four of you

You go down a beaten path and
Crawl in the wreckage
You get back on the trail
You look up all you see is a green carpet

You see only trees as tall as skyscrapers
Not a bird not a sound
These are the mighty redwood trees of
California

Conner Johnson

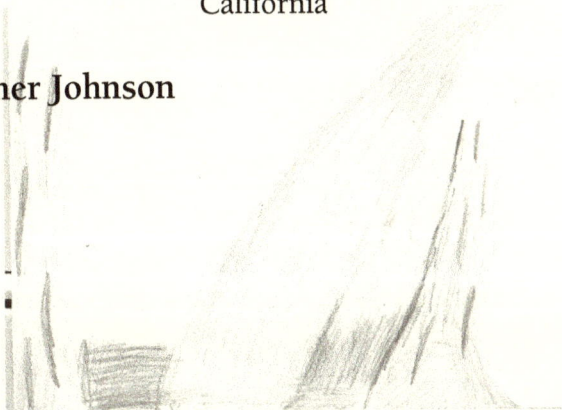

What I Am

I slither around
I have poisonous venom
I have scales

Dakota Hargrove

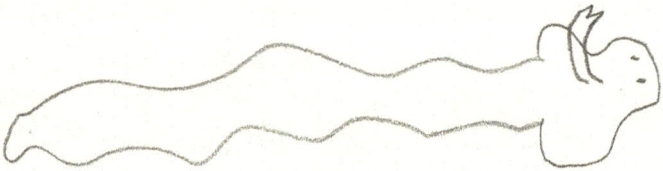

What Am I

I'm wet and scaly
I live in the ocean
What am I?

I slither on the ground
I can go in the water
What am I?

I fly high in the sky
My eggs are blue
What am I?

Jade Pearsall

In the Country

In the country you can hear a cow go moo,
In the country you can see the sky turn blue,
In the country you can feel the wetness of the rain,
In the country you can see the beauty of the day.

Kailey Kaska

My Dad

My dad
You and me
Days
And
Daddy

My Dad

Me and my teacher have so much fun,
Even at one (one 0'clock)
After that we take a nap
And then our day is over.

Kaylee Nelson

Statue Of Liberty

Oh what a sight!
The dark of night
The torch shines bright.
Like a bright flame.
Welcoming those who came.
A dream comes true
A life begins brand new.

Kellie-Ann Hovorka

Random

I'm looking at the sky while I'm eating pie.
Then I go inside and put on my tie.
Then I watch TV and I brush my teeth.
Then I get a supreme, and I say hi to Keith.
Then I put on my ski, and I go somewhere extreme.

Kleyton Benedict

Spaghetti all over!

Oh! Now there's spaghetti everywhere
What should we do?
Mom is going to be so mad.

Mom's home I'm in deep trouble
Lacey is licking it off the floor.

Kaylen and Taylor are yelling at me
I feel like I'm spinning around and around
I might as well just start cleaning up!

Kylee Marlay

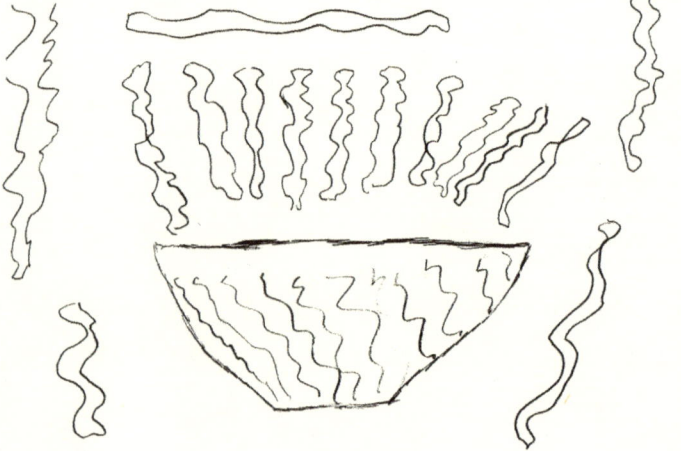

Hey diddle diddle

Hey diddle diddle a cat ate a fiddle
And choked and died OH MY
Hey diddle diddle what a sad little riddle
I can't believe my eyes

Lane Yates

Table Manners

DO THESE Rules

No kicking people
No throwing food
No being a baby
No saying I love you
No toys
No brushing your teeth
No walking on the table!!!!
AND NO BOYS!!

Maggie Ferrel

My Adventure

Once when I was in my tub
a tornado came and put me in a sub
in the ocean
it looked like a blue potion
the sub took me to a broken ship
boy it was a trip!

I swam to a chest of treasure
it was such a pleasure
then a shark came put me in its mouth
spit me out and I wound up in my tub.

Matthew McLain

The Chair

Beware of the chair,
that may give everyone a scare
It lives in a haunted house,
and for dinner eats a mouse
It is very gross and smelly,
especially when it gets Thai Deli!
Do not give it a fright!
For it may give you a bite!

Navin Martin

What to Write?

I don't know what to write?
I sit and think about it all night.
Give up, Oh, I just might.
My thoughts are all out of sight.
Now look I've spent all night.
And I still don't know what to write.

Rachel Cook

Manners and Chores

Don't burp unless necessary,
If you do, say excuse me,
Don't let the cat eat the canary,
If you do buy a new one quick,
Clean your room please, Jerry
If you don't shove it somewhere,
Do your homework, please!
You forgot! Say the dog, Merry ate it.

Ryan Pate

My Dog is Big

My dog is big
My dog is brown
But now my dog is moving
and warm.

My dog no more will splish and
Splash in mud my dog is here.

I feed my dog.

Spencer Else

If I Were A Dot

If I were a dot I would be mad and sad.
I would have nothing to do except for being bored.
I would probably get stepped on.
I wouldn't get to play with friends or go to school,
or play on the playground at school.
I wouldn't get to go to football or basketball games.

THE END

Spencer Kerr

Fat Bat

Once there was a bat
He was very very fat
He eats gnats
By a cat
And hates rats.

Alex Conrad

In My Mind

In my mind I think of flowers
Growing taller than towers

In my mind I think of bees
Making hives in trees

In my mind I think of grass
Shinier than brass

In my mind I think of the sun
That always makes me skip and run

In my mind I think of school
Which is very cool

Ben Anderson

Spring

I love spring so much
Spring is in the air today
Spring is cool to me

Brayden M. Wyatt

Sister
Nice, clean
Dancing, cleaning
Dancer, playful, weird, funny
Playing, hunting
Mean, dirty
Brother

Brooke Mclain

Money
Green and so cool
You can spend with money
I like to take money showers
I love money
Cash

Dylan Abbott

The Guy Who Lived On The Street

There once was a guy that lived on the street.
He even liked to play with people's feet.
He felt them, held them, and even smelled them.
He said they smelled sweet.
When I was about to leave he sucked them
and said "Meat"

Garrett Greiner

The Crazy Dog

There once was a dog
who acted like a dog
it loved to get treats
but it hated beets
then it came out of no where and ate a frog

Jada

Fun Fun in Branson

On Monday we saw the Presleys
We couldn't believe how they dressly

Tuesday we saw Shoji Tabuchi
He was carrying a poochie

Wednesday we saw a magician
Who made disappear a beautician

Thursday we went to Dixie Stampede
We couldn't believe the great big steed

Friday we went to the Hughes Brothers
Who were strange and didn't mind her mother

Saturday we packed up and left
Luckily our tickets we kept

Jenna Crile

Pants

Pants are on fire
A spark hit them, oh my gosh
Gotta change my pants

Jeremiah Broeg

Jeremiah
Broeg

There once was a man named Rock.
Who lived in a dirty old sock.
He was very cool.
He drooled to rule.
Then moved to a dirty old dock.

Josh Osby

My Name

Kind as a kangaroo
Yellow and black go hawks
Loves under armour
Excellent speller

Rocker at guitar hero
Oscar is my name in Spanish
Book smart
clEver as ice
Rich in friendship
fasT as lighting
Sleek as ice

Kyle Roberts

My Birthday

Birthdays Rock
Yeah
My Birthday Is Awesome please come please
I Hope You Like It, It will be fun
It's Awesome
Come
You Should Come Over Please
First We'll Open Presents
Sweet
Let's Have Fun

Logan Stark

The Old Hand

There was an old hand
That lived in the sand
It started to fight
It grabbed a bit of light
So it stayed on that old lost land

Mikaela

Mother
Clean, Sweet,
Cooking, Cleaning, Loving,
Gardening, Playing, Work, Talk
Football, Helping, Laughing
Dirty, Rough,
Father

Natalie Angstead

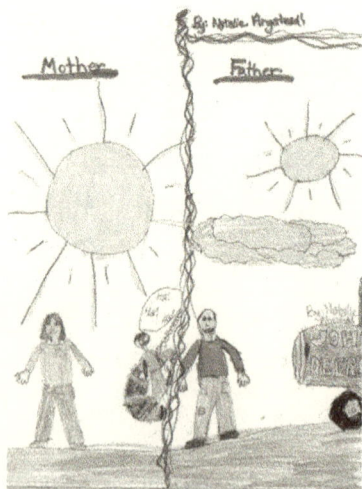

A Week of Busy

On Sunday well Sunday I went to church
And man the weather was berserk

Monday at school I played outside
Then after that I went to hide

Tuesday the creek started to flood
And all of the rain made lots of mud

Wednesday after school I went to dance
I wanted to be first but didn't have a chance

On Thursday the bus got to school late
And my mom I guess just couldn't wait

Friday we got to go to the pool
It was kind of nice to get away from school

On Saturday usually I just relax
I mean it's not like I'd pick up an ax

Paige Buch

Summer
Hot, flowers
Swimming, running, snacking
Laps, biking, shoveling, sledding
hunting, reading, fighting
Winter

Sam Fritz

The Week When Seasons Change

On Monday it was so hot
I was starting to have to blot!

On Tuesday I don't know how,
It was winter, what's going on now?

On Wednesday it turned to spring,
I don't know what's happening!

On Thursday I think I might freak,
Its fall, I see a bird with a beak!

On Friday did you hear?
It was summer winter is near!

On Saturday just like I said
It was Winter I'm going to bed.

On Sunday I think you might know,
It's spring here we go!

Sarah Swanson

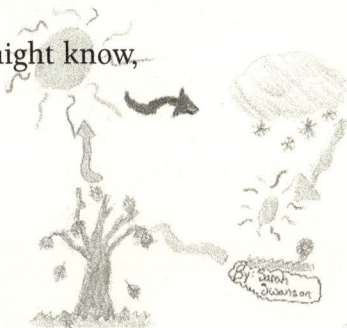

Winter

Snow falling like diamonds and crystals.
The snow is like a fluffy white carpet on the ground.
Falling, glistening, winter is beautiful.

Shado

A cat that sat on a bat

There once was a cat who sat on a bat.
But the cat got tired and stopped.
Then the bat flew up and got cut on a branch.
Then the cat wiped his feet on a mat and went
inside.

Shelby Heston

Broken Bones

Monday I broke my arm
On my alarm
Tuesday I broke my head
On my bed
Wednesday I broke my toe
On my bow
Thursday I broke my leg
And had to get a peg
Friday I broke my femur
On a lemur
Saturday I broke my foot
On a root
Sunday I broke my rib
On a crib
And now I think I'm
dying.

Simon Spalla

Simon
Spalla

Art Work
Creative Work
Drawing, Painting, Crafting
Very proud of the work I did
Fun Art

Sukhpreet Mundra

Mother
Kind, helpful
Loving, cooking, playing
Fun, happy, Smart, funny
Working, playing, sleeping
Eat fun
Father

Taylor Marlay

Once I shot a pot.
It was quite hot.
A piece of it hit my brother's pants.
No one would glance.
Then he got caught on a knot.

Tyler Huff

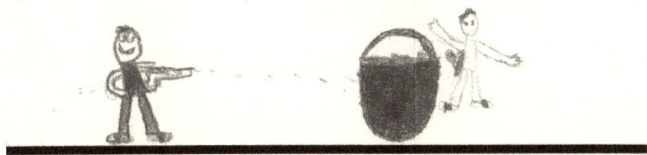

At Home

Play Games
Eat Lunch
Have Dinner
Eat Candies
Read Books
Ice Cream
Play Outside
Play Inside
Very Cool
Let's Swim
Let's Play
Have Sleepovers
Play Soccer
Play Baseball
Have Fun

Aman Mundra

Hawkeyes Rock

They're Cool
They Rock
Herkey Rocks
Good Fielding
Winning Games
Good Throwing
They're Good
Work Hard
Do Good
Very Nice

Ashley Pool

Aging

Away
Going
Into
Now
Gone

Bailey Spurgin

Crocodile

Can you see this big beast,
Floating in the water?
What is it?
A crocodile.

Brendon Lunsford

Cubs Rock

Away Winning Games
Good Batting
Work Hard
Hit Homeruns
Like Baseball
Carlos Zambrano
Derrek Lee
Sam Fuld
Kousko Fucodoma
Aramas Rimerez
Alfonso Soriano
Rich Harden
Ted Lilly
Giovanni Soto
Kerry Wood

Cade

Superman

Flying through the sky.
Saving people from villains.
Being very nice.

Cherie Anderson

My Wii

Is cool
Very fun
Looks cool
Fun games
Mario Bros.

Cole White

Heart

It is sweet.
Very nice
It is bright.
Full of love
It is great.

Fernanda Giron

Spring Rocks

Warm Days
Cool Nights
Go Camping
Go Swimming
Sing Songs
Play Outside
Feed Birds
Have Fun
Make Campfires
No Homework
Spring Break
Watch Birds
Ice Cream

Gage Hunt

Chicago Cubs

Very Cool
Hit Homeruns
Good Scores
Go Cubs!
Pop Flies
Three Strikeouts
Off Chain
Win Games
Traveling Teams
Sammy Sosa
Derek Lee
Alfonso Soriono
Center Field
First Base
Right Field
Carlos Zambrono
Chicago Cubs!

Hunter Hoskins

Hunter D.

Hyper
Understanding
Neat
Terrific
Excited
Really good
Daring

Hunter D.

Jackson

Jumping rope
Apples cooked
Cuddly cats
Koalas stuffed
September 2nd is my birthday
Outside playing with my
Noisy sister

Jackson Pohren

The Moon

The moon will come soon,
It is now night.
What a beautiful sight.

Kirsi Bland

Moon

It is bright at night.
It is very big.
The color is white.
People can go on it.
It is like a ball.
It is in the sky.

Lacy Terrell

Lisa Brimmer

I play

So cool

I'm nine

Eat food

Play games

Like math

Totally smart

I smile

Lisa Brimmer

Megan Rocks

Massive cool
Expression
Good
Awesome
Nice

Megan Davisson

Suzannah

Suzannah's my friend.
We'll be best friends forever,
Just like we should be!

Phoenix Haessler

My Friend

Really Smart

Loves Cheese

Plays Games

Very Creative

Is Nice

My Friend

Shanti Williams

The Mouse

The mouse is in the house.
My mom hit it with a broom.
I assume it won't come back again.

Sophie Allen

I Am A Little Cloud

I am a white sheep,
Walking through the sky.
I am a little cloud.

Suzannah Kingsbury

Aliegha

Art
Love
Is nice
Eats
Great
Happy
Awesome

Aliegha Kensett

Taylor

I have a friend named Taylor
She is a sailor
She is funny
but she is not a bunny

Allison Pohren

Robin

Really fast flier
Often lives in trees
Best in the wild
It lays eggs
Near my house

Andrew Alonso

Diamante

Trevor
active, fun
hunting, amazing, hitting
Fairfield, Keagan, Ashtyn, Shaylin
running, pitching wrestling
nice, goofy
Trevor

Ashtyn Drish

Richmond

Religious
Intelligent
Cool
Hunter
Mint
Our
Nice
Discover

Bowen Richmond

Diamante

Ashytn
Friendly, cool
Shopping, drawing, singing
Blue, pizza, BFF, green
Running, playing, laughing
Nice, funny
Ashtyn

Camille Schaefer

Mom & Dad

May likes March
Often reads
Must like books

Dad likes books to read
And I think he likes apples
Dad likes to play baseball

Cody Pearson

Finnegan

Friendly
Intelligent
Nice
Nuts
Energetic
Goofy
Awesome
Neat

Finnegan Mally

Mrs. Castillo

Mrs. Castillo
knows a friendly fellow
his name is Dash
because of his rash.

Graham Kuehl

Garfield

Garfield,
He lived in Fairfield
He blew up the wall
It went in the hall

Bunnar Mattson

Finn

Fire
Inside
Nice
Neat

Jose Santos

Michael

Michael
Rode his bicycle
He accidentally crashed into a tree
And then he got stung by a bee

Juancarlos Tello

Diamante

deer
brown, antlers
fighting, running, jumping
cool, fur, forest, woods
grazing, walking, hiding
huge, clever
deer

Kolten Webber

Diamante

Cindee
Fun, cool
spelling, writing, handwriting
mom, Iowa, kites, video
reading, running, loving
love, nice
Cindee

Lucia VanDijk

Mr. Blister

Mr. Blister
has a sister.
She is really bossy and mean.
She thinks she is the queen.

Macy Holderbaum

Hero

High over clouds
Even kids
Really Cool
Often have capes

Michael Flournoy

Pokemon

Pikachu
Octillary
Kukuna
Ekans
Magikarp
Omanite
Numal

Mike Dooley

Diamante

Chase
cool, funny
exciting, playing, swimming
basketball, baseball, football, outside
fighting, jumping, running
cute, fun
Chase

Nicole Buch

My Puppy Crystal

Cute
Rules house
Your attention
Sassy
Teases Jackson
Amazing
Likes blow dryer

Savannah Fleeman

Kittens

Kind
Into couches
They are cute
Terrible
Except
Nice
Sometimes rats

Shayla Spray

Lucky

Licorice
Umbrella
Chicken
Kicking balls
You

Taylor Blomme

Cotton Candy

is good
but.......
STICKY
Very, very, VERY good
I love to eat it!

Cotton Candy
Pink and blue and yellow
Sweet, sweet, SWEET
Yummy, yummy, YUMMY
In my tummy
I love to eat it!

Cotton Candy!

Alexis Kiefer

Cats

Cats
Fluffy, cute, biting
Purring and purring all day long
I want one of my very own
Cats

A'lia Martin

Recess fun!

Playing tag
Gliders
Sliding
Climbing
Football
Racing
Jumping
Recess is Radical!

Austin Adkison

139

My Brother is a Pest

OH, my brother is a pest
He runs around
And jumps up and down!

OH, my brother is a pest
He's loud and crazy.
He jumps on the bed,

OH, my brother is a pest
But as a twin brother….
He's the BEST!

Blair Bowman

Basketball

Basketball
Dribbling, passing, shooting
I always play it in my backyard
Basketball is my favorite sport
Basketball

Brenden

Winter

Winter is cold
When I play outside.

Winter is boring
When I'm inside.

Winter reminds me
Of vanilla ice cream
It is all white and cold!

Brian Parcell

Principal's Office

I'm in the principal's office,
Shaking like crazy.
I'm nervous
He might give me detention,
For a week, or a month, or a year.
But why am I nervous,
It's only my imagination.

Carson Crile

Home Work

Boring
Not fun
Wastes time
Too much
Too often
Too much math
Too many pencils
Too much learning
I wish there was no more!

Carter Spalla

Baseball

Running, hitting,
Catching, throwing, pitching,
Stealing, sliding, cheering, clapping
baseball

Chase Lathrop

Kassidy

Kassidy is my sister
Awesome
So cute
So much fun
Is funny when she runs
Dogs are her favorite animal
You will like her!

Cierra Kinsey

Cody's Tooth

Cody's
Loose tooth fell out
Three days ago at school.
(Now a new tooth will grow in that spot.)

Cody

Eggs

Big egg
Little egg
Silly egg
Colorful egg
Beautiful egg
Gross egg
Great egg
But most of all
Easter eggs!!

Collin Breen

Owls

Big great horned owls
Little elf owls.
Brown barn owls.
White snow owls.
Mean owls.
Calm owls.
Quiet owls.
Scary owls.
Funny owls.
Awesome owls.
Baby owls.
Fluffy owls.
Owls are interesting!

Cooper Drish

S is for…

S is for salamanders.

Salamanders are silly and

Small s is for snakes.

Snakes slither.

S is for Seals.

Seals have soft skin.

S is for salamanders,

Snakes, and seals.

Delanie

Molly

Molly likes to run
Molly likes to have fun
Molly likes to sleep
And never makes a peep
Molly is magnificent!!!!!!!!!!!!!!

Mia

Pizza

Pizza
Cheesy, spicy, flaming hot.
Makes me want more and more and more
I think it's the best kind of food.
Pizza

Nickel Iseman

Lions

Live in Africa
Incredible cats
On dry pride lands
Not pets
Special to me

Sam Mattson

Sharks

Sharks, Sharks,
Sharks eat meat.
Sharks, Sharks,
Sharks swim fast.
Sharks, Sharks,
Sharks eat anything
Sharks, Sharks,
Sharks eat other sharks.
Sharks, Sharks,
Sharks live in the ocean.

Seth Mickels

Easter

Easter
fun pretty colorful
Makes me happy to find easter eggs
I hope I will get lots of candy
Easter.

Shelbie Long

Sisters

Sisters can be
Fun!
They can also be
A PAIN!!!
Its fun to have
A playmate,
Especially
When there's
Nothing
TO DO!!!

Sophie Elliott

Horses

Horses are my favorite animals.
Once I rode a horse with my mom.
Running, trotting, galloping, walking.
Some horses are very fast.
Everyday I go out and pet my horse.
Some day I will ride a horse in an arena
  and I will feel happy.

Tyler Heston

The Wet Wackerdoodle

Mr. Snickerdoodle had a Quckerdoodle
Who had a Wackerdoodle
Who loved to take showers
So he could smell like a flower
Oh, that wet Wackerdoodle!

Dylan Smithburg

Fony Jony

Jony was a Fony
She was the Ancient Mummy covered in honey
From Egypt.
She was a ghostly post who got all the candy
From Mandy.
She ate peanut butter in the car
From a jar.
She did her math
In a bath.
But…Jony was still a Fony

Rhylie Lisk

Fifi Bonini

One day during a test
(It was not the best)
A little girl named Fifi Bopini
Walked in like a sweetie
She ate her lunch
With a "munch, munch, munch"
Then looked at her grape and said,
"It's not in shape"
She threw it on the floor and said,
"I'll get more"
Fifi Bopini was not a sweetie!

Lura Gamrath

Goofy Goob

Goofy Goob ate good grub.
When he got full
He stuffed his grub in the tub
Then he went to bed
To rest his head
He heard a big boom
And saw some elves in his room
He chased them out with a frown
All the way to town
They will never come back again!

Brittan Bowman

Plum the Drum

One day Plum the Drum got hit by some sauce…
It was thrown by his boss
"Accident," said his boss.
Cheer the Geer said, "It's alright,"
So frightened was Plum the Drum
He dropped his gum.

Nicholas Frisbie

Hummy Mummy Came to School

Hummy Mummy was a great big bunny
She had a big doll
And loved to eat gummies
One day she came to second grade
And sat on my desk with her doll on her lap
I let her stay till she ate my gummy.
Then I got mad and said, "Go away Hummy Mummy."

Olivia Roberts

Jummy Crummy Came to School

Jummy Crummy came to school
He ate his lunch and drank his punch
He thought he was cool
Then he took the test....and made a real mess
He was a monkey...it was ok, I guess.

Henry Smith

Animal Family

Nog the Frog had a dog and a hog
A cat and a bat
An eel and a seal
And a pig with a wig.
He used the eel to peel
Bananas from Montana
What a weird family of animals
They all went to heaven
Nog looked at his seven
And said, "My, my it is bright up here!"

Hunter Parish

Bed Head

Bed Head went to sleep
And woke up with messy hair
It was always like that
His very best friend was Red Head
Who had red hair
NOT messy hair like Bed Head.

Jackson Weaton

One Silly Day

Pepper Clepper ate pizza on a plate
He said it was pretty cheap to keep
When Pepper Clepper got home
He dropped it on the lawn
And said, "It's all gone"
Pepper Clepper couldn't wait
Till eight to go the hill
To have a party!

Jillian Dunlap